2/15

Pebble® Plus

Cool Robots
ANIMAL ROBOTS

by Erika L. Shores

Consulting Editor: Gail Saunders-Smith, PhD

Consultant: Seth Hutchinson, PhD
Department of Electrical and Computer Engineering
University of Illinois

CAPSTONE PRESS
a capstone imprint

Pebble Plus is published by Capstone Press,
1710 Roe Crest Drive, North Mankato, Minnesota 56003
www.capstonepub.com

Library of Congress Cataloging-in-Publication Data
Shores, Erika L., 1976– author.
  Animal robots / Erika L. Shores.
     pages cm.—(Pebble plus) (Cool robots)
  Summary: "Simple text and full-color photographs describe eight different robots that mimic animals and the work these robots do."—Provided by publisher.
  Includes bibliographical references and index.
  ISBN 978-1-4914-0588-8 (hb)—ISBN 978-1-4914-0652-6 (pb)—ISBN 978-1-4914-0622-9 (eb)
1. Robotics—Juvenile literature. 2. Robots—Juvenile literature. 3. Technological innovations—Juvenile literature. I. Title.
TJ211.2.S539 2015
629.8'92—dc23
                                                                                    2014002310

Editorial Credits
Terri Poburka, designer; Katy LaVigne, production specialist

Photo Credits
Cheetah Robot image courtesy of Boston Dynamics, 7; Courtesy AeroVironment, Inc., 19; Getty Images: AFP/Kim Jae-Hwan, 5; Newscom: AFP/Getty Images/Toshifumi Kitamura, 11, Reuters/Morris Mac Matzen, 21, WENN.com/BigDog image courtesy of Boston Dynamics, cover, 13, ZUMA Press/Zhang Jun, 9; Science Source: Brian Bell, 15; Virginia Tech: Amanda Loman, 17

Design Elements
Shutterstock: Irena Peziene, Kate Pru

The author dedicates this book to Mike, who likes robots but not animals.

Note to Parents and Teachers

The Cool Robots set supports national science standards related to science, technology, engineering, and mathematics. This book describes and illustrates animal robots. The images support early readers in understanding the text. The repetition of words and phrases helps early readers learn new words. This book also introduces early readers to subject-specific vocabulary words, which are defined in the Glossary section. Early readers may need assistance to read some words and to use the Table of Contents, Glossary, Read More, Internet Sites, and Index sections of the book.

Printed in China
032014   008085LEOF14

Table of Contents

Animal Robots 4

On Four Legs 6

In the Water 14

In the Air. 18

Glossary 22

Read More 23

Internet Sites. 23

Critical Thinking Using
the Common Core 24

Index 24

Animal Robots

Scientists who build robots study real animals for ideas. A robot's tail helps it swim like a fish. Wings on a robot make it fly like a bird.

On Four Legs

Cheetahs are the fastest animals on land. Scientists built the Cheetah robot. It can run 29 miles (47 kilometers) per hour.

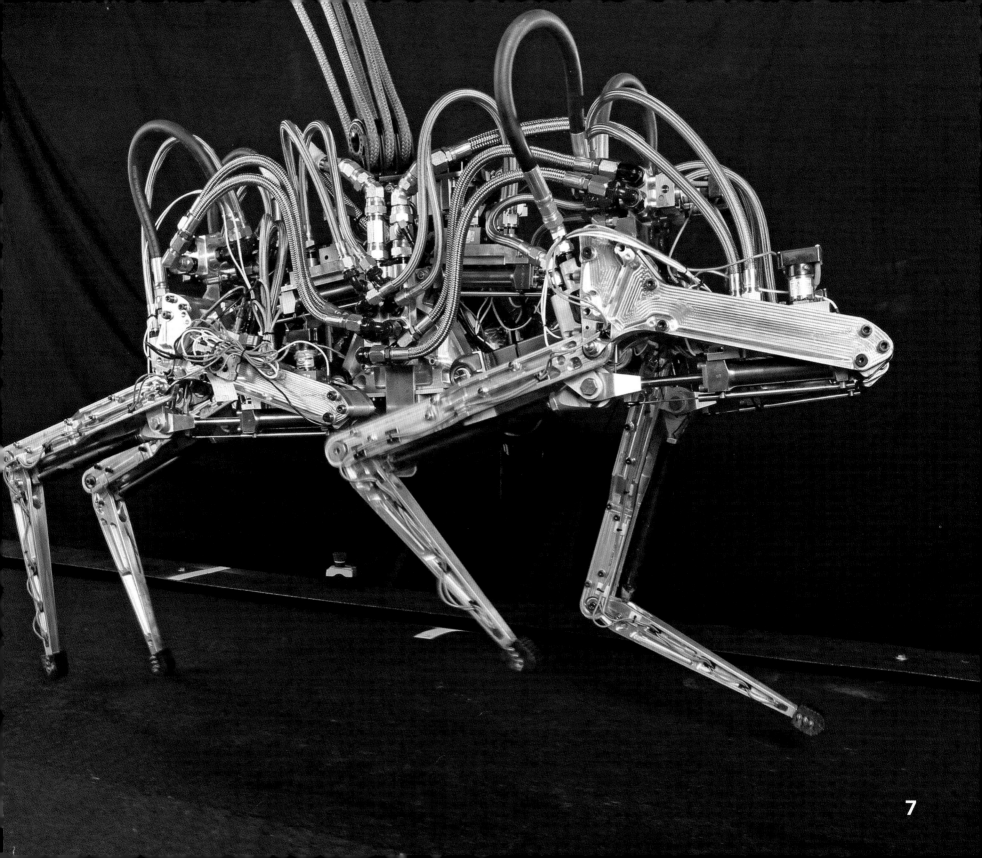

Would you like a pet dinosaur?

Pleo looks like a mini dinosaur.

The robot sings, dances,

and follows commands.

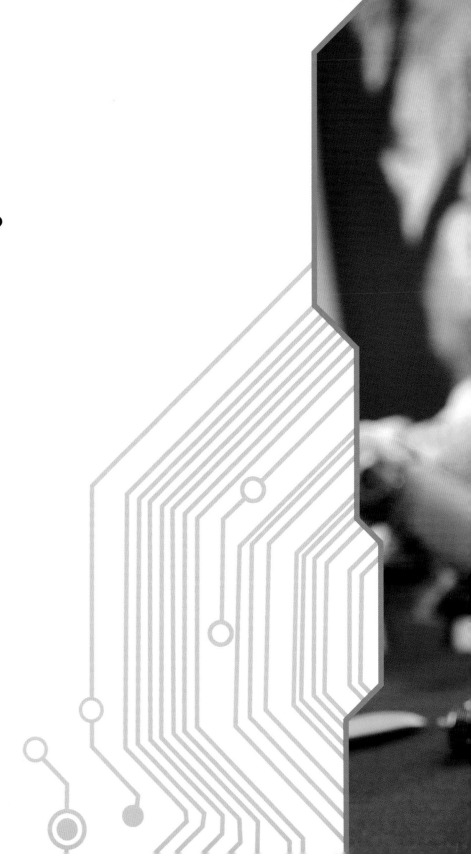

This little dog won't eat
your homework.
AIBO understands 100 words.
A camera in its head
allows it to chase a ball.

11

The BigDog robot can walk through mud, snow, and water. It does this while carrying a load of 340 pounds (154 kilograms).

In the Water

A robotic fish is made to swim in oceans. It searches for pollution. The robot's computer sends information to scientists on land.

Cyro is a robot that looks
and acts like a real jellyfish.
Someday Cyro could be used
to study fish and other ocean life.

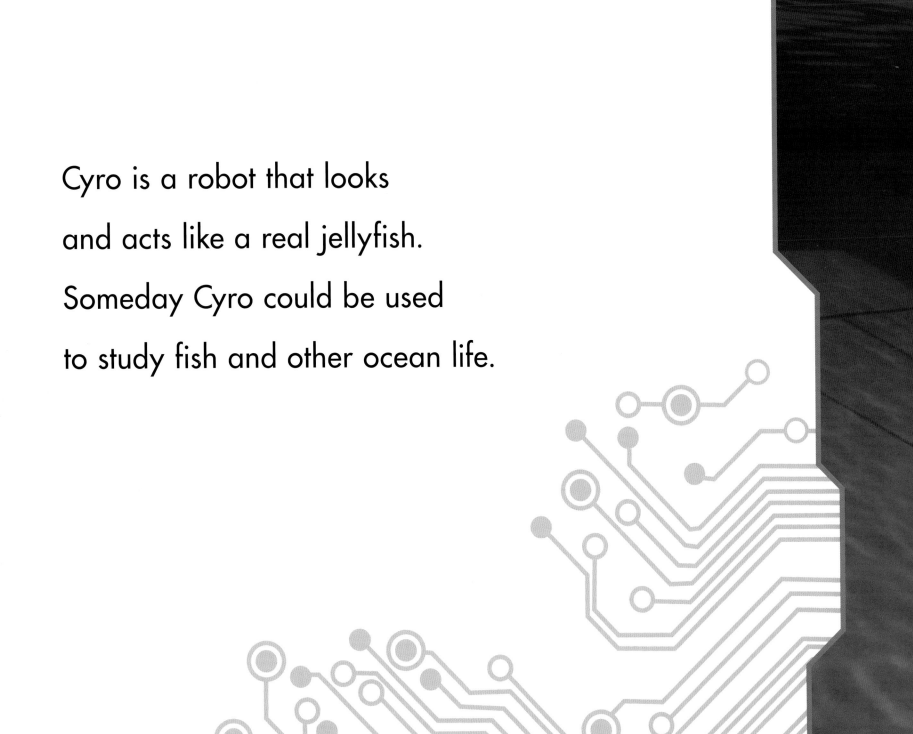

In the Air

The nano hummingbird is a flying spy. The U.S. military plans to use this small robot to gather enemy information.

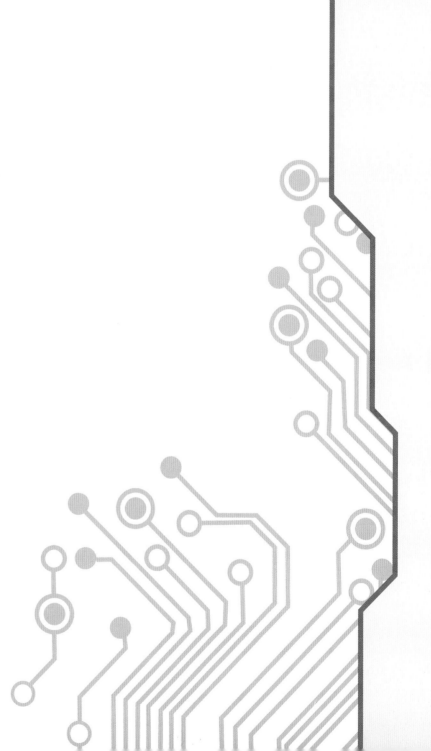

This bird doesn't need feathers to fly. The SmartBird robot flaps its wings to take off, fly, and land on its own.

Glossary

command—an order to do something

information—facts and knowledge

pollution—materials that hurt Earth's air, water, and land

robot—a machine that can do work and is operated by remote control or a computer

scientist—a person who studies the world around us

spy—to watch something closely from a hidden place; a spy is a person or machine that gathers information secretly

Read More

Alpert, Barbara. *Military Robots.* Military Machines. North Mankato, Minn.: Capstone Press, 2012.

Brasch, Nicolas. *Robots of the Future.* Discovery Education: Technology. New York: PowerKids Press, 2013.

Internet Sites

FactHound offers a safe, fun way to find Internet sites related to this book. All of the sites on FactHound have been researched by our staff.

Here's all you do:

Visit *www.facthound.com*

Type in this code: 9781491405888

 Check out projects, games and lots more at **www.capstonekids.com**

Critical Thinking Using the Common Core

1. Look at the photo on page 19. Describe why this robot might make a good spy. (Integration of Knowledge and Ideas)

2. Describe ways in which BigDog is a useful robot. (Key Ideas and Details)

Index

AIBO, 10

BigDog, 12

cameras, 10

carrying, 12

Cheetah, 6

commands, 8

computers, 14

Cyro, 16

dancing, 8

flying, 4, 18, 20

nano hummingbird, 18

Pleo, 8

running, 6

scientists, 4, 6, 14

searching, 14

singing, 8

SmartBird, 20

spying, 18

swimming, 4, 14

tails, 4

wings, 4, 20

Word Count: 200

Grade: 1

Early-Intervention Level: 17